Peeling The Onion

Printed in the United States of America
Published by Donna Marston

D1160900

Table of Contents

3

Dedication

I dedicate this book to my oldest son for finding his way into recovery and to those who continue to support him and each other in the Fellowship of a 12-Step Program.

To all of the Mothers, Fathers, Husbands, Wives, Children, or anyone who is hurting because you love a drug addict or an alcoholic. I hope that you will have the courage to live your life on life's terms to learn to live in the solution not the problem and find the strength and faith to heal your heart!

Acknowledgements

A warm and loving thank you to Barb C. . . Barb is an addiction Counselor who is also an amazing woman. Barb's words of wisdom, kindness and love impacted my son's recovery and our family. We hold Barb near and dear in our hearts, she is our Angel.

I thank my husband for educating himself about the disease and loving our son unconditionally and I am grateful for our thirty two years of marriage.

I thank my youngest son for his love, support and being the wonderful young man that he is.

I thank my older son for finding his way into recovery and keeping his promise of becoming a better man.

I thank my family and friends who supported me through some of my darkest moments.

Acceptance

If I want to be accepted as I am, then I need to be willing to accept others as they are. We always want to have our parents accept us totally, and yet often we are not willing to accept them as they are. Acceptance is giving us and others the ability to just be. It is arrogant to set standards for others. We can only set standards for ourselves. And even then, we want them to be more like guidelines than standards. The more we can practice self-acceptance, the easier it is to drop habits that no longer serve us. It is easy for us to grow and change in an atmosphere of love.

"Louise Hay – How to Heal Your Life".

Chapter 1

INTRODUCTION

My name is Donna M.; I am a Mother of a recovering drug addict/ alcoholic. This book is about my journey of healing and what I learned through the years of my son's addiction and recovery. I decided to share my experience because when I let go of my secret, I was amazed at how many families are affected by this disease.

My intent for writing and sharing this book is to pay it forward in hopes that my experience and knowledge will benefit someone who is dealing with a loved one who is afflicted by a horrible disease called drug addiction or alcoholism.

Before I go into my story and tell you who I am, I would like to tell you a little bit about what I do. On April 21, 2011 I spoke in front of the New Hampshire Senate Finance Committee. I read a testimonial asking the Committee not to cut funding for Health and Human Services. I know firsthand that Rehabilitation Centers work for recovery and that they are necessary in today's society; my son is a living example that they work.

I currently speak at a couple of rehabilitation centers in New Hampshire every month for Family group sessions and on occasion I will be asked to speak at a various functions. Six months out of the year, I write for a Southern N.H. newspaper about enabling and co-dependency. Although I don't have the allergy, I have experienced the 12 steps as they are laid out in the big book with my Step Study Sponsor and with the God of my understanding. I want to make one thing perfectly clear; I'm not your typical Author, I'm not a Philosopher, Psychiatrist, Psychologist or a Drug and Alcohol Counselor; I'm a Mom who had a broken heart and who found my passion and my voice.

<u>What I will and will not tell you</u>

I will tell you about the lessons that I learned, while dealing with a drug addict in my family. I will talk about my process of healing and the tools I utilized along my way. I will not tell you about every little detail of the crisis and drama that we went through as a family for two reasons. The first and most important reason is that I respect my son, his recovery and his anonymity and if he wants to tell his story, he can, I am only willing to share with you my knowledge and feelings. The second reason is that if you are reading this book you already know what dealing with a drug addict or alcoholic feels like; therefore, I don't feel that we need to compare notes.

Our stories may be different or they could be exactly the same, but in the big scheme of things the story doesn't matter. What matters is that our emotions are the same. We are hurting, we live in fear, we are angry, depressed, and all we want is for our loved one to stop drinking, drugging or both.

I will tell you that:
1. Letting Go and Letting God is huge for all of us to do.
2. Refusing to play the victim or being a martyr is freeing.
3. Taking back our power is uplifting.
4. Not participating in their craziness, drama or crisis is peaceful.
5. Connecting to our Higher Power is healing.

Over the years I learned that there isn't a right or wrong way, it's finding the way that works best for us personally. Everyone has different needs, wants, results and experiences. Do what works best for you according to where you are in each moment.

I learned to take the story of the situation while allowing myself to feel my emotion. When we repeat the story to whoever will listen, or constantly repeat the story in our head, all we are doing is stirring up the feelings and hurting ourselves emotionally.

For example: If my son verbally abused me, and I allow myself to constantly think about his words, I continue the story. If I remove the story from my thought process or don't repeat it to anyone who will listen, I'm letting it go. I have the right to my feelings; therefore, it is important to identify them.

The way I deal with this is that I envision I am holding an empty box; I put the story inside the box, tape it up and remove it from my thought process. I then identify my emotion and breathe through it, when I'm done feeling it; I release it to my higher power.

Chapter 2

<u>Who Am I?</u>

I am a Mother who is recovering from depression, a broken heart, living in fear of my son dying from abusing drugs. I am recovering from the anger and the financial toll that was created from my son's addiction.

I am a Mother who was desperate for answers of how to save my son from drugs and myself from depression. I am a Mother who was quickly losing her son to the disease while I became addicted to saving him.

I was a stay at home Mom, Den Mother, P.T.A. Board Member. I was active in school fund-raisers and activities that involved my children. My husband worked long hours so when the boys were entering into their adolescent years he decided to take a job that would give him the flexibility to be home more so he could help raise our boys, coach them in Baseball, Basketball. My husband always stated that he didn't want to watch his boys grow up on video; therefore, he changed careers for five years, so that he could be more involved with them from grade school through their middle school years.

My husband and my intentions in raising our children was to love and support them unconditionally (*not to suggest that we never got upset with them or never made mistakes*), to teach them accountability, manners, to respect others and have good work ethics. We felt that our job as parents was to groom them to become productive, functioning adults. We were involved parents, so what the hell went wrong?

I am not trying to make my husband and me out to be perfect parents, I don't believe that anyone is perfect but my point is, whether you're a stay at home Mother/Father, hands on parent(s), working parent(s), no matter what your parenting skills are, social status is or financial status, **addiction has no boundaries!**

For years my thinking about addiction is what I choose to call innocent, ignorant because I thought that drug addicts were criminals, or homeless people begging on the street corner for money. I had a vision in my head that was completely and utterly wrong! I learned that there is another side of drug addiction that I never considered, I have been humbled.

Re-evaluating my Mothering skills

I wish I could tell you that being so involved with my son's childhood made a difference in who he became as a teenager. When I found out that he had a serious drug problem in his early-twenties, I was devastated, numb, and sick to my stomach. I wasn't completely blindsided about his drug use, because I did suspect for many years during his teen years that something was wrong, but I just couldn't figure it out. I would often question him if he was using drugs and of course he would be so offended that I would dare ask such a thing and on occasion I would go through his room looking for any sign of drug paraphernalia.

When the truth finally reared its ugly head, I felt the need to re-evaluate how I mothered him. Some of the thoughts that swirled around in my head for a very long time were: Did I love him enough? Was I too strict with him? Was I a bad Mother?

After months and months of beating myself up as a Mom, I came to realize that my son's drug addiction had nothing to do with me and here is why I came to that conclusion:

I didn't cause it: I didn't introduce my son to drug dealers, I didn't crush the Oxycontins so he could snort them and I most certainly didn't shoot heroin into his veins so he could run away from himself, I didn't cause his addiction period!

I can't control it: Now that I have educated myself about the disease, the odds of me controlling my son's drug addiction were as good as the odds would have been if I jumped out of an airplane while in flight without a parachute and believed that I would land on my feet unharmed.

I can't cure it: Thinking I could cure him was me playing God, I'm not that powerful, I can love him and be his biggest cheerleader but I can never cure my son of anything.

For those of you who love a drug addict or an alcoholic I just described to you the three C's of codependency.

Codependency is unhealthy love and the tendency to behave in overly passive or excessively caretaking ways that negatively impact one's relationships and quality of life. It also often involves placing a lower priority on one's (*our*) own needs, while being excessively preoccupied with the needs of others "Enable" or allow the person to continue his or her self-destructive or troubled behavior (*Wikipedia encyclopedia*).

Codependency is when we make a relationship more important than we are to ourselves. It doesn't mean that it is a one sided relationship; it's a relationship where a co-dependent person is trying to make the relationship work while the other person isn't working at it.

10

The substance abuser or alcoholic may have trouble controlling their impulses; they may not show much interest in the relationship while the co-dependent person goes all out trying to repair the relationship or the problem.

The codependent person may feel that they are the better person or think that they have it all together. A co-dependent person may define themselves as being strong enough to deal with their loved one's addiction.

A typical co-dependent person will attempt to rescue or protect their loved one who has gotten into trouble with their family, work related issue's or the law. I have learned that you're co-dependent if you put your loved one to bed if they have passed out. You're codependent if you make up excuses for him or her; you're codependent if you call in sick to their work, you're co-dependent if you pay their bills. A co-dependent person will typically take care of the finances, while trying to hold the family together and especially attempting to preserve the family image.

I thought by loving my son more, co-signing whatever he needed me to co-sign and giving him money would be reason enough for him to stop doing drugs. It took me ten years to realize that I needed to stop my co-dependent behavior and take care of myself emotionally instead of thinking that I could save my son from his addiction.

If you are co-dependent and you have been doing the same behavior over and over and over again while expecting a different outcome, then it's time to try something different! Change your behavior, thought process and get emotionally healthy.

I'm As Sick As My Secret

Oh, how emotionally sick I got while loving the addict in my family. I remember one day feeling that I should stand naked in front of my home to let everyone who knew me, know that my life is a lie. *"Oh, but I can't"*, I thought to myself, and in that pivotal moment, I also realized that I have a secret and I felt in my gut that you don't share these kinds of secrets with just anyone. I thought to myself, *"Oh, my God! What the hell am I going to do now?"* The tears began to flow; and the gut wrenching pain in my stomach was unbearable, I felt like I was going to die. Off I went into the fetal position, I felt depressed, defeated, and then there were days, I didn't even know if I had a feeling inside of me, because I felt numb. There were days that I truly felt that if I didn't die from a broken heart I was going to end up on some Psychiatric ward.

My thoughts became tormented, if I reach out for help, people would know my secret and if I continued to keep my secret, I risked staying stuck on my emotional roller coaster ride to hell.

For years, I only told two good friends and a few family members about my son's drug addiction. I didn't want anyone to know that my son was a so called drug addict. Why? Because I was ashamed and embarrassed that I had a drug addict in my family and more importantly and painfully, it was my son. When I first learned that my son was abusing drugs, all I did for hours, days and months was cry, and if I wasn't crying I was researching drug addiction, I was constantly looking for answers. I wanted answers that would explain my son's behavior or how I could save him from drugs. I was so pre-occupied with saving my son, that I was slowly losing myself.

When the depression set in, I would go from my bed to the living room couch to the family room couch. I went round and round for hours, days and months. I couldn't control my pain, I couldn't eat, I couldn't sleep and I couldn't concentrate on anything but my child. In other words, I became addicted to saving my son; and he became my drug of choice.

When I finally got off the couch and out of my bed, I figured I'd research his behavior. My computer became my new best friend. I would be on it for hours upon hours researching drugs and addiction.

Did you know that you can buy clean urine on-line? Wow! That was amazing to me not only was I educating myself, I could not believe the drug paraphernalia that is sold legally in stores or on-line. There are items designed specifically to look like every day ordinary items. I found high-lighters that hide a small pipe, a lipstick tube, where the ends come off and it becomes a pipe and a fake cigarette that hides a pipe. Who the heck thinks of these things?

I was hoping that my new best friend (my computer) would help me find information that would explain my son's behavior. It began to dawn on me that the child I thought I knew wasn't who I thought he was. I was so obsessed with saving my son from drugs that he became my drug of choice, in other words I became addicted to saving him.

I learned the Serenity Prayer:

"God, grant me the serenity
to accept the things I cannot change;
courage to change the things I can;
and wisdom to know the difference."
Reinhold Niebuhr

There is such a stigma to addiction and that is why I thought that if I kept my secret (*keeping up the family image*), everything would be ok. I eventually learned that I was as sick as my secret because as long as I kept it, I remained emotionally paralyzed living in fear of social judgment.

My son's first re-habilitation center was at a local outpatient facility; every Tuesday night was family night. The first night my son asked me to attend, I remember feeling so angry at him, "*why did he put me in this situation, now I have to show my face in a public situation and worst of all why should I have to go sit with those people*"? No wonder I was fearful of judgment, I too was judgmental. I thought anyone who had a drug problem must be a criminal, homeless or just some low life.

I have since learned that when we point our finger at others we should take a look at the three fingers that are pointing back at us. We often accuse others of their bad behavior while we deflect our own.

When I walked into the room that night, I was never so humbled. I saw people who looked like they could be a family member, friend or business associate of mine. I learned that night that addiction has no boundaries! It doesn't matter what you're social, financial or family status is addiction affects all of us. We are all coming from the same emotional place, our hearts are aching, our stomachs are in knots, we're angry, we're sad, we feel defeated. All everyone in that room wanted was for their loved one to stop drinking or drugging.

I wanted to scream at all of the patients "*Just stop using, damn it! If you love your family, you will stop, if you want a good job, you will stop and if my son really loved me, he could stop. Please love me enough to get healthy, PLEASE, PLEASE, PLEASE, JUST STOP using drugs! I'm here because I love you and I know you can do it, all you have to do is say NO!*"

I eventually learned that just saying no, is not as simple as it sounds when someone is lost in their addiction.

Over time I began to share my secret, it was very freeing! I learned that I have nothing to be ashamed of, bottom line my son is sick. I wouldn't be ashamed or embarrassed if he had cancer or diabetes. Therefore, I should not be ashamed that there is a drug addict in my family because addiction is a disease; it's an allergy of the body and an obsession of the mind.

When I began to speak freely and openly about my son's disease, over the course of many years, I learned that I was not alone. There are so many families struggling with a loved one who is addicted to drugs or alcohol.

God Grant Me The Serenity

After reading the Serenity Prayer over and over and over again, I began to dissect it so that I could attempt to understand how this prayer could help me survive this craziness.

God grant me the serenity to accept the things that I cannot change: This statement was telling me that I should accept that I cannot change my son's behavior or choices that he makes. My debate (*in my head*) was this: *"I'm his Mother, for the first eighteen years of his life, I told him what to do, how to do it and when to do it and now, I have to let go, are you kidding me?"* As much as I did not want to accept this, I had to realize that my son was a young adult and it was time to let go and accept that I could not change him. His journey in life is his journey, not mine.

Courage to change the things that I can: I can set healthy boundaries, I don't have to enable him and I can give myself permission to take care of my own emotional and mental health.

And the wisdom to know the difference: Sometimes this got a little convoluted for me but when I started to come out of the darkness, clarity started to shine through. I learned to listen to my gut not my heart.

Throughout the years I found it difficult to step back and let things be, I would always re-act to his behavior. If I didn't like what he was doing or saying I would go for the juggler saying things to intentionally hurt him, hoping that I would get a reaction from him that would make him stop abusing drugs and I wanted him to stop lying and to be honest with me. I can tell you first hand that this tactic does not work! It took me years to understand that if he couldn't be honest with himself about his drug use and lifestyle, he certainly couldn't be honest with me or anyone else; therefore, all I did was stir up the drama. He'd get angry, I'd get angry, we would both say hurtful things that we couldn't take back and really didn't mean. The end result of those arguments was justification for him to go and get high and then he could put the blame on me. For example: *"Mom, if you had just given me the gas money so I could have put gas in my car so I could have gone to work, I wouldn't have to had to get high."* This is what I like to call deflecting their accountability and believe me; they are very good at this, blaming others for their own recklessness.

My son once told me that he was a drug addict because I didn't buy him designer clothes when he was in sixth grade, not for one second was I going to own that accusation!

Tough Love or Unconditional Love

I heard stories from parents who practiced tough love and it didn't work for them, so I had to do what I thought what was right for us. I believe that there isn't a right or wrong way; it's finding your way.

I chose what I thought was unconditional love, because through those sensitive years, that is what worked for me. I couldn't bear not knowing if he was dead or alive, therefore, I never kicked him out of our family home although there were many times I threatened too, I just never meant what I said back then. I thought that tough love meant turning my back on my child, sending him packing and never speaking to him until he hit his bottom. I now know that tough love is sticking to the agreement or healthy boundaries that we set for ourselves and with our loved one.

I have come to believe that substance or alcohol abusers are often broken people. It is my opinion that something in their journey of life broke them, it could have been something that was said to them, they may have been bullied, someone may have been sexually, verbally or emotionally abused, or it could have been as simple as their lifestyle catching up with them. My son's breaking point started in sixth grade because he was bullied. I personally find that many of the people who are affected by this disease are very sensitive; they have good souls, with kind hearts that are broken.

So here's what I struggled with: If I have something or someone in my life that I love, that's irreplaceable to me; I would find a way to repair the item or the relationship. If I have a disagreement with a family member or friend, my normal reaction would be to resolve the situation because I love them. So why the hell can't I love my son unconditionally without judgment and save him from his addiction?

Throughout the years that my son was using, we would make agreements, if I co-signed a car loan(s) or school loan(s); he promised me that he would stop using drugs. I chose to believe him and I believed if he was happy, he would do better in life. Take my advice on this; do not attach your name to their debt, for two reasons: #1. My son didn't pay his bills, therefore, his debt, became mine and #2. It's enabling. I also allowed him to stay in our family home because I needed to see him on a daily basis, I needed to know that he was eating, that he had a clean bed to sleep in and most important that he was alive, I believed at the time that I did this for me, not for him. I could not bear the thought of my son being out on the streets doing God knows what. The healthy boundary I should have made with him was he could live in my home as long as he was drug free, held a job and paid his own bills.

I have learned that there is a very, and I mean a very fine line from choosing unconditional love versus enabling and becoming co-dependent. For years I had them confused. I now know from experience that a drug addict or alcoholic have to do their own work to get clean and sober, they have to want it for themselves. Substance abusers can't often survive on their own, which is probably why they attempt to keep us engaged in the dysfunction, that being said, I do believe that they need a support system. As a loved one, we can't buy them enough or love them enough to make them stop; this disease is so much bigger than all of that. Enabling is doing for your loved one, what they could and should be doing for themselves.

<u>An Open Letter To My Family</u>
(This was a handout at one of the re-habilitation centers that I speak at)

"I am an alcoholic. I need help.

Don't solve my problems for me. This only makes me lose respect for you.

Don't lecture, moralize, scold, blame or argue, whether I'm drunk or sober. It may make you feel better, but it will make the situation worse.

Don't accept my promises. The nature of my illness prevents my keeping them, even though I mean them at the time. Promises are only my way of postponing pain. And, don't keep switching agreements; if an agreement is made, stick to it.

Don't lose your temper with me. It will destroy you and any possibility of helping me.

Don't allow your anxiety for me make you do what I should do for myself.

Don't cover up or try to spare me the consequences of my alcoholism. It may reduce the crisis, but it will make my illness worse.

Above all, don't run away from reality the way I do. Alcoholism, my illness, gets worse as my drinking continues, start now to learn, to understand, to plan for recovery. Find Al-Anon, whose groups exist to help the families of alcoholics.

I need help – from a doctor, a psychologist, a counselor, from a recovering alcoholic who found sobriety in Alcoholics Anonymous, and from God. I cannot help myself.

Your Alcoholic"

Do I Love My Son The Drug Addict Or Do I Hate Him?

Being Raw and completely honest, there were many days that I honestly didn't know if I loved or hated my son. I felt that I hated him because I was paying his bills, I hated him because I had to bail him out of jail, I hated him because he lied to me, I hated him because he stole from me, I hated him because I paid off drug dealers and I hated him because my family was falling apart. In the big scheme of things, I hated that I was enabling him; therefore, I needed to take responsibility for my actions and stop blaming him for what I allowed because I had a choice. Back then I thought the more I did for him and the more I paid his way, I was helping him. I justified what I thought was being the perfect Mom! Truth be told, I wasn't, I was enabling and co-dependent. Instead of letting him suffer the consequences and be accountable for his behavior, I let my fear and his disease control me.

The hate in my heart caused me guilt and shame, how do you hate your own child? What I eventually figured out was that I did love my son, but I hated the disease. The disease was destroying my son, me and my family because we all somehow adjusted to living with dysfunctional behavior. I realized that my son had become my drug of choice, I was addicted to saving him and at that time I would do whatever I deemed necessary to do so.

When we love a drug addict or alcoholic, they become the main focus of our attention and disruption in our lives. We often face many emotions and obstacles while dealing with a loved one's addiction that often causes us frustration which creates anger within ourselves. We tend to blame ourselves, we try to fix (*control*) them, we engage in their drama and eventually our love for them feels like hate.

It took me years to learn that I should not punish my son because he was abusing narcotics, and didn't like his behavior, nor should I rescue him from his consequences by bailing him out of jail or paying off a drug dealer.

Dealing with my sons addiction became a very lonely place for me, the silence became very loud as I isolated myself. I eventually realized that I needed to educate myself about enabling and co-dependency, get myself emotionally healthy and reach out to people who have walked my walk.

Broken Heart
By: Donna M.

My heart is clearly broken and I don't know what to do, I have fought with my emotions to keep on loving you. I have lived in denial of what you have tried to hide, but now I know you have awakened that tiger deep inside.

I look at my beautiful boy whose emotions are stuffed so deep within, your emptiness, and self-worth, I'm wondering how the hell it all began?

The battle of your addiction you just can't disguise, trust me I'm your Mother, I can see it in your eyes.

Your lonely lost and broken and I cannot save your soul, damn it! If you would just let your demons go, you just might become whole.

I can no longer fight the tiger that has taken you away, because it's bigger than I ever knew, therefore, I commit to no longer enabling you.

I pray for strength and hope to survive the hell that you have put me through and I pray that one day you'll return the son that I once knew.

The Battle that family members fight when we love a drug addict or an alcoholic is horrific! As a Mom, I thought trying to fight the disease was doable, I found out the hard way, it isn't. The tiger (*I refer to as the disease*) is so much bigger than all of us.

As a Mom, I know the gut wrenching pain that we endure when our child is lost in their disease of addiction. Many of us believe that it is our job to save our children, to protect them from themselves, the poor decision that they make and we attempt to protect them from the consequences of their disease.

So many of us struggle with how do we turn our backs on our children and let them suffer the consequences in hopes that they will reach their bottom and get help. Believe me, when I tell you, it is not your deal! I too struggled with this, I blamed myself for years, was I too strict, did I love him enough, did I treat him differently than his younger brother and the answer is no to the majority of my questions and yes, I loved him with all of my heart. The bottom line is that no matter if I loved him more, bought him more, and enabled him more, it did not stop him from continuing to use drugs and creating his unmanageable life, fact is, my enabling probably kept him engaged in his disease longer. I learned that his disease wasn't about me, that I didn't have to take it personally, his disease was about him, and he had to figure out his demons. I could however, be his biggest cheerleader, love him and support him emotionally, have compassion for him without expecting anything in return. I then can respect myself by setting and sticking to healthy boundaries.

I fought this battle for years and as time passed, his disease was progressing and I had less and less fight in me. I don't know if that was because I felt defeated or I was learning to let go and let God!

A Letter To My Son

4/28/2008

"I wish I could put a band aide on your pain like I use to when you were a little boy, a kiss and a hug, would make the pain go away. I know that your pain is so much bigger than what a band aide and a kiss can heal. Unconditional love doesn't even work.

All your life I believed in you, fought for you and loved you more than I ever thought I could love anyone. I wish you could love yourself that much.

I'm so sorry for you, that the drugs have interfered with your life. I hope that one day you will love yourself more than the drugs. I hope that one day you will see what a beautiful person you are and I hope that one day you'll believe in yourself enough to never use drugs again.

The torment must be horrible for you, one can only imagine. The torment for your Dad and I sometimes is unbearable but we choose to continue to believe in you because we do have faith that you are stronger than your demons and the drugs.

I pray that you never lose complete control but then again maybe hitting your rock bottom will be what makes your life important enough to save.

With all my heart I love you!

Mom

Chapter 3

<u>What I Have Learned</u>

I have learned that alcoholism and drug addiction is a disease, I use to believe that it was a choice; all my son had to do was decide he wasn't going to use drugs. I really thought it was just that simple until I saw a documentary at his first re-habilitation center called *"The Sleeping Tiger"*.

The narrator used a flip chart while explaining the disease. He began by showing how each of us has a sleeping tiger cub in our stomach (*gut*) that grows as we grow, through childhood, adolescence and into adulthood. The Tiger sleeps within us until that one day that we decide to take a drink or experiment with drugs. If we are vulnerable to the disease, we wake the Tiger. The more the substance abusers drinks or uses drugs, the bigger the Tiger becomes until the Tiger is in control and the person is lost somewhere within. The Tiger is the disease of alcoholism and drug addiction.

I also learned that every time a substance user decides to stop abusing drugs or alcohol and enters into recovery, the Tiger goes back to sleep. If they relapse, they do not go back to the first day that they ever picked up their first drink or drug of choice; typically they will go back to where they left off because they have re-activated their addiction. Every time my son relapsed his Tiger got bigger and bigger until his life became unmanageable and out of control.

At this point, it's starting to dawn on me that my son might be sicker than I know; maybe this isn't a phase that he's going through. I'm also beginning to realize that there is nothing that I can do, I can't shelter him enough, I can't nurture him enough and no matter how much I show him that I love him, it's just not enough! This disease is so much bigger than I could have possibly imagined.

Years later while visiting my son at yet another re-habilitation center; I came across the AA Big Book. As I thumbed through the pages, I came across this statement *"Addiction is an allergy of the body and an obsession of the mind"*.

The disease of drug addiction and alcoholism is a progressive illness. I have learned that it can't be cured, however, they can be in recovery and that there is a solution if they chose to seek it. Recovery is probably where the slogan *"One day at a time"* came into play. There were days where I felt my life was one breath at a time or one minute at a time.

Allergy of the Body and an Obsession of the Mind

"Alcoholism is an obsession of the mind that condemns one to drink and an allergy of the body that condemns one to die."
-- Dr. Wm. D. Silkworth

A non-alcoholic can have a drink, maybe two, and if they start to feel tipsy or a sense of being out of control, they typically will stop. An alcoholic will have a drink and begin to feel more confident, or in control. Another drink will only increase the feeling so another will be needed after that and then another and another until they typically either pass out or blackout. When a person crosses that line of social drinking into alcoholism, they may never be the same again. So bottom line here is, once an alcoholic puts a drink or a drug addict puts drugs into their system it sets off a craving for more.

Imagine layers of an onion, the first layer is the way their body reacts to alcohol or drugs when they ingest it, that's the craving and the second layer is the insanity of the mind just before they have that first drink or drug. Until they get to the root of why they are self- medicating and why their lives have become unmanageable, will they find their way to sobriety.

The Stigma of Addiction

I recently read that the American Society of Addiction Medicine came out with an updated definition of addiction, which identifies five other aspects: inability to abstain consistently, impairment of behavioral control, cravings, diminished recognition of significant problems, and dysfunctional emotion responses.

I have learned that society has a tendency to create labels and stigmas when it comes to referring to a person with an addiction problem. The Merriam-Webster dictionary defines a stigma as "*a mark of shame or discredit*". Society seems to think of drug addicts or alcoholics as being weak.

A person who is in active addiction is often called a junkie or a drunk and these words are a label that is demeaning to another human being. It is important that society learn to make a distinction between the person and the disease and change the negative language used when referring to a person suffering from substance or alcohol abuse.

People in active addiction often continue to use drugs or drink alcohol to numb their emotional pain. Guilt and shame are probably two of the reasons that keeps them self-medicating. It's a shame that society doesn't often have respect for a person who enters into a re-habilitation center so they can learn how to deal with their emotional pain and their addiction.

Society has a tendency to profile people; therefore, it probably doesn't give much thought to the popular cheerleader or the all-star athlete in high school who is good looking, smart, and has a great personality as a drug addict or alcoholic, who drinks alcohol or pops a pill to take the edge off every morning before he or she arrives to school. Do you think society profiles the professional business man or woman who goes off to their full time job every day in a business suit as a drug addict because he or she is successful? Professional people often project that they have a wonderful life, because they have a good job, a nice family and live in a desirable neighborhood. But little does anyone know that the stress of their job or keeping up their image has become too stressful. One day he or she takes a pill to take the edge off, likes the way it makes them feel, and if they have the ism, they wake the tiger and the disease eventually causes a lifestyle that becomes uncontrollable.

I have learned that people can and do become addicted to prescription medications and just because a Doctor prescribes them the addiction isn't anything less or more than someone who uses street drugs, but perhaps it's easier for them and society to justify.

In my opinion substance abuse has become an epidemic in our society and no one is immune because addiction has no boundaries! It doesn't matter what your social, family or financial status is.

What I Have Learned About Addicts/Alcoholics

I don't believe that a person who is in active addiction wakes up one day and says to themselves or anyone else: *"I think I'll mess up my life up today and become addicted to drugs or alcohol so that I can get myself arrested, enter into the legal system so that I can create a life of hell for me and my family"*. I learned that they are biologically or otherwise vulnerable to the disease.

I learned that my son while active in his addiction became the most convincing liar, manipulator and thief that I had met in my many years of life. He could look me in the eye; swear on my soul that he wasn't living the life that I suspected he was living. He was so convincing that for years I thought that I was the crazy one.

I learned not to believe a word that came out of his mouth, to listen to my gut. I learned that when I believed in him, that was my hope and that was all I had in that moment.

I learned that I could not control his addiction and I could not control his behavior but I could control how I re-acted to it and I could control whether I stayed stuck in the craziness.

I learned not to attach my name to any of his debt. My son would promise sobriety, if I would just co-sign a loan for a car or school.

I learned he couldn't stay true to what he promised because his money went to self-medicating, therefore, he never paid his debt and it became my responsibility.

I learned not to let him use my debit/credit card to purchase gas. I thought that by letting him use my card, I could monitor my account as a backup of what he was doing. Truth be told even though the receipts matched my bank account, I eventually learned that he would meet his drug dealer at the gas station, fill the dealer's car with gas in exchange for drugs and give me the receipt. It was tough to swallow that I was paying for my son's drugs that could have killed him. I also learned that they can use our credit cards to take their dealers out to eat, to the mall, to the grocery store; they can use our credit card for just about anything in exchange for drugs.

I learned his behavior. I would watch for mood swings, when he was loving and sweet (*his voice went up a few octaves*) he was typically high. When he was cranky and nasty, blaming me for everything that was wrong in his life was when he was drug sick.

I also learned that he got acne and would pick at his face when actively using. He began to look dirty and disheveled. His pupils were like pin heads and his eyelids were heavy, his mouth would hang open with drool running out the side of his lips, and he would nod off. Years into his addiction, he had a horrible smell to his body and in his room; I learned that was the smell of heroin oozing out of his pores.

I learned to hide anything of value. I cannot stress this enough, they will take whatever they know a dealer will take in exchange for drugs or they will take the item(s) to a pawn shop in exchange for cash.

I learned that I should not keep alcohol or any form of medication in my home. If they need to self-medicate, they will use whatever is available to them. Barb C. my son's counselor at his last re-habilitation facility asked me *"do you have alcohol in your home?"* I answered, *"yes, but it has been there for years, it's only used if we have company"* she responded with *"your son is an alcoholic, he is allergic to alcohol. If your son was allergic to strawberries, would you have them in your home?"* I debated with her that my son was not an alcoholic; she then stated *"your son can never drink again because if he does, it will weaken his senses and eventually he will go back to using drugs"*. My son understood this concept and he will tell you that he is a recovering drug addict/alcoholic, alcohol being his second choice if he can't get drugs. It took me some time to come to terms with this label but I can now say that *"my son is a recovering drug addict/alcoholic"* with no shame or emotion around it.

I learned that if my son ever needs to have blood taken, that he should have someone who is safe go with him, the reason is that the needle going into his vein could be a trigger for him to go back to shooting up heroin.

I learned that when a person is active in their disease, they have no boundaries when it comes to taking our belongings. I don't believe that their intent is to hurt us, they are sick and need to self-medicate and they will take from us whatever they can to sell in order to get money to feed their addiction.

I learned that my son didn't have to live up to my expectations. My hopes and dreams for my son are my expectations that I put on him. My son can only live up to his own expectations.

I learned that relapse happens. It is not uncommon for our loved ones to relapse. They can try to stay drug free or sober but if they go into a treatment center to please us or get us off their back, they more than likely will have a prescription to use as soon as they get out. They have to reach out for help for themselves, because they want to live a better life on life's terms, not our terms.

I learned that my son's recovery was his full time job and none of my business. Every time my son came home from a facility, I would be on him about getting a job, owing me money, going to meetings. I was toxic to my son, and he could use me as a reason or justification in his mind why he relapsed.

I learned to "Let Go and Let God" because this disease was bigger than anything that I had ever experienced in my life.

Signs of Drug Abuse and Addiction

It is often difficult to imagine that someone you love, a friend, or co-worker could be using drugs or abusing alcohol. There are many warning signs of drug addiction that can range from what may seem to be harmless judgment on their part up to being arrested, going to prison or dying.

For years I suspected my son was using drugs but he would always have an explanation that would seem reasonable and throw me off. As time went on, I knew in my gut that something was very wrong; it took me years to catch him in his lies. When my son first admitted to using drugs he initially told me that he was addicted to Oxycontin, years later the truth was that he was a serious heroin addict.

Over time I noticed that he looked dirty, he didn't care about his appearance or his cleanliness. He would nod off with drool sliding out of the side of his mouth, he was disengaged. He had scabs on his face, he was constantly picking at himself. Eventually I noticed an indescribable odor from his body and in his room. A friend of his told me that it was the smell of heroin oozing out of his pores. He would be up all night and could sleep all day. He was extremely thin and his behavior was erratic. My son was slowly dying and we all knew it and there was nothing that we could do to help him because at the time he didn't want our help and he was too sick to help himself. He thought that he was in control of his addiction when in fact; his addiction was in control of him. It's a horrible thing for a Mother or anyone else to watch.

If you suspect that you have an addict/alcoholic in your life, here are signs to look for (info from Narconon): **Signs of Alcohol Abuse:** Breath smells of Alcohol, Eyes unusually bright, Illogical talk or behavior, sleeps late, hidden bottles or cans. **Prescription Drugs:** Appears drunk, slurred speech, stumbling, and droopy eyes. **Opiate Abuse:** Pinpoint pupils, needle marks in arms, wears long sleeved shirts on a hot day, sweaty and thirsty, nodding off, and drooling. **Cocaine Abuse:** Constantly sniffing may have no appetite, use very powerful lighters, grouchiness, illogical talk, sleeps late, crushed or burned cans. **Meth Abuse:** Erratic behavior, broken teeth, weight loss, may sweat profusely, scabs on arms, face, legs, sleeps late after no sleep, broken glass, light bulbs. **Marijuana Abuse:** Bloodshot eyes, dazed appearance, slurred speech, suddenly very hungry, illogical talk, sleeps late, blank stare.

If you suspect that someone in your life has an addiction problem, don't ignore the signs, reach out for help.

What I Know To Be True

I know that most if not all drug abusers and alcoholics cause a lot of stress, drama, crisis, sleepless nights and quite often a financial decline in their lives and ours.

I know that while living in the drama or crisis of our loved one's addiction, we hurt, we want to fix them, and we want them to stop their self-destructive behavior and we can't.

I know that I didn't have to play a role in his mess.

I know that I am not a victim.

I know that living in my head can be my hell.

I know now, that I was powerless over my son and his addiction.

I know that he was hurting himself and I was allowing myself to be hurt.

I know that he blamed others for his addiction while never looking at himself.

I know that he didn't wake up one day and decide to become a substance abuser.

I know that we both had to find our way through the journey of his addiction.

I know that there is a light at the end of the tunnel because I found it.

I know and understand why people will give us advice whether we ask for it or not. They will make judgments or hurtful comments. We have a choice to listen and believe what they say or take what we need and leave the rest behind.

Please Keep Your Opinion To Yourself

Dear family and friends,

I truly want to believe that you mean well when you offer advice of how I should or should not handle the drug addict/alcoholic that I love. You think that you are helping me when you share your thoughts of how you or someone you know would handle my situation and you tell me you know what I'm feeling.

Well, here is what I have to say to you: Your opinions, judgments and criticism are often hurtful. You don't know how or what I'm feeling as these are my emotions, not yours. You may think you know what you would do if you had a child or a loved one who is affected by this disease, bets on, you won't take your own advice. Bottom line, what goes on between my son and me is really none of your business.

When you over step your boundaries with me, I will isolate you, I will resent you and I will lash out at you verbally because you have triggered an emotion within me that I have yet to heal.

You don't want me to take your constructive criticism personally; then please don't take my reaction to it personally.

I am doing the best I can, I am emotionally fragile, I am living in fear, I have a broken heart and at the moment I am a lost soul just like my son is. My pain wreaks havoc with my mental state because I am fearful and that fear brings me to my knees. I deal with so many emotions that people who aren't living what I'm living, won't typically understand. I have to do what I have to do until I am sick of being sick - just like the drug addict/alcoholic that I love. When I've had enough of feeling like I'm the crazy one is when I will reach out for help so until then, I'm on a long, raw emotional roller coaster ride and I'll get off of it, when I'm ready.

If you really want to support me then listen to what I have to say, without judgment or criticism; sometimes I just need to vent. If I want your advice, I will ask you for it; don't gossip behind my back, it's hurtful. Let me cry, scream or do whatever I need to do in your presence because you may be my safety net in that moment. I am holding on to my hope because that's all I have right now, so please have patience with me.

Respectfully,

Donna M.

Chapter 4

Addiction Affects Relationships

A person who is active in their addiction is often selfish and their goal is to continue using drugs or alcohol. They often use relationships as long as it promotes their ability to continue to self- medicate. If someone close to them reacts to their hurtful behavior, they will typically put up walls to isolate themselves in order to protect their disease.

Some relationships in recovery can be a bit of a double-edged sword. Of course they are necessary and they can provide us with joy and fulfillment in many different ways, but at the same time, relationships can be somewhat dangerous, especially for the newly recovering drug addict or alcoholic.

One of the biggest stumbling blocks, especially for young people, is letting go of their old friends that they use to drink or get high with. This can be especially tough because in many cases, these people are actual friends, not just friends who they use with. Every time my son came home from a re-habilitation facility, he was lonely; he knew he needed to meet new friends that were living a clean life but because of his loneliness, he would go back to hanging out with his friends and it was a matter of time before he relapsed. When my son came home from his last facility, this time he befriended some of the old timers at meetings and eventually he met young men his age and he has now established wonderful sober friendships.

Sober Siblings Are Entitled To Their Feelings

Everyone in the family has a right to their feelings, it's all in how we express them and treat each other.

As the years moved forward my oldest son's addiction was progressing and the relationship between my two boys was falling apart. Aggression set in and communication was just about non-existent.

Our sober children have also been lied to, have had their money and material items stolen, they may be embarrassed or ashamed of their brother or sister. I was told by a friend who has a sibling that is a drug addict: *"My experience was all the attention went to the addict and his bad behavior. The rest of us were non-existent except for listening to the ranting and raving and having the frustration taken out on us"*.

Sober children don't often have the coping and verbal skills that an adult has. We are their role models, the problem is that we are trying to survive emotionally and as the parent(s) we must tread carefully.

I can only share with you what worked for my family:

* Keep the lines of communication open with your sober children and be their safety net.

* Let them express their feelings without criticism or judgment.

* Be their role model, children learn from our behavior.

* Educate them that about their siblings addiction and consider counseling.

* Don't put all your attention on the addict in your family.

Moms often ask me how they should intervene with adult siblings. Scenario: Sober sibling refuses to attend a family function if their brother or sister who is actively using is attending the event. Mom is trying to diffuse the situation because she loves both kids and wants her family to be together. When my youngest son would refuse to attend a family function I would say: *"I am sorry that you feel that way, I certainly understand and respect your decision".* You can leave it at that or add *"we will miss your presence, and if you should change your mind, which I hope you do, we would love for you to be with us."*

A. You're not allowing yourself to be in the middle.

B. You're being respectful to his or her feelings.

C. You're not creating or playing into any drama.

D. You're not trying to control the situation.

If you're sober child stands by his or her decision, than stand by your statement to respect them, otherwise don't say what you don't mean.

The Toxic Dance

Engaging in our loved ones toxic behavior creates drama and crisis in all of our lives. In my opinion engaging in what I call the toxic dance is why our lives also become unmanageable and out of control.

Years ago my son came to me very upset that one of his drug dealers was after him and that he needed nine hundred dollars to pay his debt, otherwise this person was going to hurt him.
My fear set in, I allowed myself to get caught up in his drama.
I debated if I should give him the cash knowing that I was enabling him or risk that this dealer may physically hurt or possibly kill him. After stewing about this, I chose to pay the debt because I knew that I couldn't live with myself if something happened to him

37

over money. I found out later in his sobriety, that he actually only owned the dealer five hundred dollars, so guess where the other four hundred went?

I learned that when my son and I made agreements with each other, we both had a tendency to move the finish line. I made threats that I didn't mean or was afraid to put into action for fear that I would lose him.

The toxic dance is another form of enabling which is the process that family members, partners, parents, children or friends, "enables" a drug addict or an alcoholic to continue to drink or drug by failing to set healthy boundaries, by failing to recognize the problem and or by participating in their behavior.

Could You Call The Police On Your Loved One?

There were times that I threatened to call the police on my son, but he never pushed the issue far enough that I had to make that choice. Looking back, I used idle threats as a form of discipline while I was living in the craziness of his drug addiction. I don't think that it is fair to call the police as a form of discipline because in my opinion, it's our job to parent our children, not theirs. If I'm being completely honest with you, I'm not sure that I could have followed through if he chose to ignore me because I lived in so much fear and one of my biggest fears was that my son would be arrested and end up in prison.

It's a tough, gut wrenching decision because what parent wants to risk having their child go through the court system and I guess in the big scheme of things, it would have been giving up my control over to law enforcement. If your loved one continues to drink or drug, they'll typically end up in the court system all on their own.

If your loved one is causing harm to themselves or others or if you know for sure that they have committed a crime, that is when you should call the police.

Don't make idle threats, our children or loved ones will eventually see through them. It's very important to mean what you say and say what you mean, so take the time to think things through before you speak. You cannot solve your loved ones problem and don't cover up their actions to spare them from the consequences of their behavior.

<u>The Three Consequences of Addiction</u>

Addiction is unconscious behavior; a person typically is self-medicating to dull their pain. There are three major consequences that many drug addicts and alcoholics will probably encounter due to their behavior while drinking or drugging - Time in jail-prison, Rehabilitation Center-Physiciatric Ward or Death.

Out of the ten years that my son was using he encountered being arrested two times. The first time he was in jail for the night and I bailed him out as soon as I received his call. The second time he spent a weekend in jail, only because I wasn't allowed to bail him because he was in another state and they would not release him on bail until he went to court the following Monday. I couldn't stand the thought of him being in jail, I put fear around the situation and created stories in my head of what could happen to him while incarcerated. Believe it or not, if you're love one *ends up Homeless* ends up getting arrested **DO NOT** bail him or her out. I eventually learned that the best thing we can do is to let our substance abusers spend time in jail. If no one comes to rescue them, they will hopefully feel the loneliness; have time to think about how there life has become unmanageable or out of control and it might be their rock bottom that gives them the strength to seek help in hopes of finding sobriety. My son never got arrested again after spending a weekend in jail.

My son also checked himself into one outpatient and four inpatient Rehabilitation Centers over the course of his last four or five years of using. On family day I was there as soon as it began and left at the very last minute that I could. I could not bear to think of my son sitting alone while other families were visiting their loved ones (*typically, he was one of the few who had visitors*). I would bring him new clothes, food (*if allowed*), whatever he requested I brought it; in hopes that it would make him happy, and as comfortable as he could possibly be. I would call him daily just to hear his voice to know that he was ok. Notice all of the I's? I wanted him to be happy; I wanted him to be comfortable. It wasn't about what I wanted or needed it should have been about his wants, needs, and choices and most importantly his sobriety.

There is a fine line of being supportive versus enabling and I crossed all of the lines. It took me years to understand that by enabling (*doing for him what he could and should do for himself*) my son, I was not allowing him to fully suffer the consequences of his actions and in the big scheme of things, I was helping him to continue to stay addicted to drugs and an even scarier thought is that I was helping him to slowly kill himself.

Drugs and alcohol will rob them of their minds, their bodies and eventually their life!

__Why Do Substance Abusers Lie and Manipulate?__

Drug addicts and alcoholics have a tendency to lie and manipulate in any relationship to support their addictive behavior. They falsely justify that they have to lie or manipulate us because in their sick minds we are way too controlling or act unreasonably toward their right to drink or abuse drugs.

I found that my son seemed to be twenty steps ahead of me, it was hard to catch him in his lies and I made myself crazy trying to do so. Family members and friends often feel stressed, betrayed, hurt, and angry and victimized because we have been duped by them so many times.

My son could easily manipulate me because I lived in fear of him dying. He could look me square in the eye and swear on my life that he was telling me the truth and if I questioned his actions or words, he would verbally assault me. For example: If I would ask him to take a drug test, he would get crazy mad, calling me names, accusing me of not trusting him and he would eventually storm out of the house without taking the test. Over time I learned to pay attention to his reactions to my questions. If he went ballistic and started verbally attacking me, I knew he was using and I was his scape goat to get himself out of the uncomfortable situation.

They may love us but they love their drug or drink of choice more when they are actively using. Their behavior is often confusing to us, it leads us to become very suspicious of anything that they say or do. Their goal is to manipulate us with shame. What they typically accuse us of is a mirror image of their behavior. Drug addicts or alcoholics typically will blame us while they don't or won't own their own bad behavior. Their disease is in control while they are lying and conniving.

If you are currently dealing with a loved one and their addiction, may I suggest that you don't believe a word that comes out of his or her mouth? They will say or do anything that will give them access to your money and believe me when I tell you that if they can't be honest with themselves, they most certainly cannot be honest with you.

When they get sober, they often regret their behavior; feel shame and remorse for what they put themselves and us through. In their sobriety some may be frustrated that our trust is gone, they don't understand why we still feel hurt but what they need to understand is that before we can believe or trust them ever again, they have to walk the walk of sobriety because their words mean nothing to us anymore. Trust is earned and it takes time!

The Fake Pleasure of Addiction

Anyone who has had a drink(s) or experimented with drugs at one or more times in their lives has probably felt empowered. For example: Many people who aren't addicted won't get up to dance until they have a couple of drinks under their belt, typically it's because drinking will allow a person to feel more confident in a social environment. I don't have the disease but I can tell you that when I was younger and use to drink, I was one of those people who would never step foot on a dance floor without having a couple of drinks, why? Because I would loosen up and could let myself go. Knowing how I felt with a drink or two, I can certainly understand how a drug addict or alcoholic loves the feeling of empowering fake pleasure.

A true addict or alcohol starts off having fun in a social environment, but eventually they go will go overboard and their behavior will typically cause them embarrassment or trouble. Once the disease kicks in, they will be chasing the drink or drug of their choice until they hit their rock bottom. What once empowered them could ruin their lives and the relationships with the people who love them.

During the years of my son's drug addiction he would tell me that he wasn't hurting anyone but himself. He was so wrong; he was hurting his family and everyone who loved him while he was slowly self-destructing. Substance abusers and Alcoholics have no clue and to be perfectly honest, they don't really care when they are actively using about the impact that they have on their family and friends. My son would also make the statement that *"if you had my problems you would use drugs too"*. That statement was my son playing the victim role because I didn't need to self-medicate to stop the hurt, worry and fear that his addiction was causing me to feel. Fact is his problems were complicated by his addiction, because he self-sabotaged his own life by choosing to live a negative lifestyle. As his Mother, I learned that there was nothing that I could say or do to stop him from using. Intuitively he knew the right path to get clean and sober so that he could embrace a better version of himself.

A drug abuser and an alcoholic are in serious denial if they continue to drug or drink while they are suffering serious life consequences such as loss of employment, driver's license, freedom and their family due to their addiction. Alcoholics and drug addicts can be best described as those who continue to use, even when they have clearly suffered a loss due to their addiction.

Drug addicts and alcoholics seem to rise to the challenge of being selfish *(Having regard for oneself above others' well-being. wiktionary.org/wiki/selfish)*.

Take Me in Your Arms

So now, little man; you've grown tired of grass, LSD, acid, cocaine and hash. And someone pretending to be a true friend said, "I'll introduce you to Miss Heroin."

43

Well, Honey, before you start fooling with me, just let me inform you of how it will be. For I will seduce you and make you my slave; I've sent men much stronger than you to their grave.

You think you could never become a disgrace, and end up addicted to poppy seed waste. So, you'll start inhaling me one afternoon; you'll take me into your arms very soon.

And Once I've entered deep down into your veins, the cravings will nearly drive you insane. You'll need lots of money (as you have been told) for, Darling I'm much more expensive than gold.

You'll swindle your Mother, and just for a buck, you'll turn into someone vile and corrupt. You'll mug and you'll steal for my narcotic charm, and feel content when I'm in your arms.

The day you realize the monster you've grown, you'll solemnly promise to leave me alone. If you think that you've got the mystical knack, then, Sweetie, just try getting me off your back.

The vomit, the cramps, your gut tied in a knot, the jangling nerves screaming for just one more shot. The hot chills, the cold sweat, the withdrawal pains, can only be saved by my little white grains.

There's no other way and there's no need to look, for deep down inside you will know you are hooked. You'll desperately run to the pusher and then, you'll welcome me back into your arms again.

And when you return (just as I have foretold), I know that you'll give me your body and soul. You'll give up your morals, your conscience, your heart; and you will be mine, till death do us part.

"Anonymous Addict"

The Evil and Corroding Thread

One of the evil and corroding threads that substance abusers, alcoholics and the people who love them often feel is fear.

Is fear false evidence appearing real or is it the absence of love? I personally think it can be both. By definition fear is: An emotion, generally considered negative and unpleasant, that is a reaction to a real or threatened danger *(Mosby's Dental Dictionary, 2nd edition. © 2008 Elsevier, Inc.)*.

In my personal experience, my fear brought me to my knees. I was fearful that my son would be beaten by a drug dealer, arrested, go to jail or prison, and the most crippling fear of all was that he would end up dying from a drug over dose.

Through the many years that my son was actively using drugs I could and did create all kinds of stories in my head that in turn stimulated my fear. Fear can touch every aspect of our lives if we allow it to, mine kept me paralyzed where I couldn't work, eat or sleep and from experience; I can tell you that it isn't a good place to be. I eventually learned that I had a choice, I could continue to live in fear or I could surrender it because, I could not control how my son chose to live or what the end result would be.

For the drug addict or alcoholic some of their fear may be driven by the absence of love. When I've gone to meetings of the fellowship, I often hear members say now that they are in recovery; they are learning to love themselves.

Six months into my son's recovery, he was doing so well, had a great new job, made lots of new sober friends so I decided to ask him why his recovery was working this time. He looked at me with his beautiful sparkling blue eyes and told me that he was learning to love himself.

Relapse Happens

In an article that I read about relapse years ago stated that relapse rates for addictive diseases range from 50% for resumption of heavy use to 90% for a brief relapse. My son was in five re-habilitation centers and within hours, days or a few months after leaving each facility, he would relapse. In his sobriety he has told me that he would have a prescription to use before he even left the facility, in other words he went through the process to appease me but knew it was a matter of time before he would get high. A thirty day program just wasn't enough for him; his last time in a facility he did a ninety day in house program and he did it for himself.

Although time is an important factor in their recovery, the reality is their mindset. In early recovery their mind slowly start to clear but the fog has yet to be lifted. I have been told that it takes up to a year for their brain to start to heal from the damage that drugs and alcohol can cause. If an addict/alcoholic doesn't have the basics of how to stay clean and sober, it's probably inevitable that relapse will happen. Addiction and alcoholism is an allergy of the body and an obsession of the mind.

There are probably many reasons why relapse happens depending on what is going on with your loved one; here are some of the most common factors:

1. **Cravings:** The physical compulsion and mental obsession. Cravings are probably one of the most contributing factors because typically they are physical or psychological.

2. **Losing control:** After having time in recovery, it is not uncommon for an drug addict or an alcoholic to think that they

can drug or drink socially and if they do, it's probably a matter of time before they go back to where they left off.

3. **Socializing with the same friends:** It is often difficult for them to adjust to sober living and meeting new friends.

4. **Stress:** Typically a drug addict or alcoholic will self-medicate as a way to deal with their stress.

When relapse happens, they typically feel guilt and shame, it's important for them to find preventable resources and learn the tools that are proven to work.

There are many symptoms to look for to identify when your loved one has relapsed, such as: weight loss, exhaustion, dishonesty, frustration, self-pity, depression, being impatient, acting cocky, or taking an "It can't happen to me attitude" or concentrating on the problem instead of the solution. One red flag with my son was when he would often wear his dark sunglasses in the house.

A drug addict or alcoholic must be willing to allow time to pass, as they will need to endure the temporary discomfort and most important, incorporating a positive attitude toward their recovery because recovery is their new full time job.

Chapter 5

Has Your Life Become Unmanageable and Out of Control?

If you answered yes to this question than it's probably time to re-evaluate your life. When you're ready to admit that you are powerless over your addiction or trying to save your loved one from addiction, it is critical to realize that you can't do it alone.

Whether you have the allergy to the disease or not we all must enter into the path of recovery. This is when we let go, we surrender our will and control to a higher power, something greater than ourselves to a God of our understanding.

My son was brought up Christian but through the years of his drug abuse, he became agnostic. He felt that if there was a God, he wouldn't be living in pain or in his destructive life style. There were times that I too questioned God. *"Why would God allow this to happen to us? We're a good family, we treat people with respect".* The answer that would typically pop in my head would be "why not?"

In my spiritual awakening, my higher power as I understand him that I choose to call God, does not judge, criticize or make life difficult. I have learned and believe that when bad things happen in life, typically it's because one human being is doing or has done something to another human being or that I made a poor decision. Instead of looking at ourselves, I feel that we often use God as a scape goat.

During my son's last time in a re-hab, he refused to say the name God, instead he called his higher power Dude, and that is who he prayed to for a long time. He now gets on his knees every morning before starting his day and prays to the God of his understanding.

Whether you have the disease or not if you are seeking help but don't think that you can work with the idea or name of God than consider this, G.O.D. - good - orderly - conduct.

The act of surrendering is really letting go of our ego, I choose to call my ego my lower self. Typically our egos are what get us into trouble because it's often fear based, lack of trust or controlling behavior. When we all learn to deflate our egos we will find serenity and peace which leads us to our higher self. Surrendering is an act of faith that allows us to get out of our own way and let things happens the way they are meant to be.

There are many programs available to anyone who is ready to Let Go and Let God.

Just Maybe
By: Donna M.

Maybe someday your life will be as awesome as you pre-tend it is.

Maybe the biggest lesson in our lives is
how we value relationships.

Maybe we are here to unconditionally love a person who is afflicted with the disease of addiction.

Maybe we are here to love ourselves which may
free ourselves from addiction.

Maybe the value of achieving sobriety is in the achievement.

Maybe life isn't about creating you, it's about finding yourself.

Maybe gratitude is when your memories are stored
in your heart, not in your mind.

Maybe one day at a time is enough.

Maybe looking back at our past will give us
the opportunity to clean up our future.

Maybe you can't change your past
but you can change your future.

Maybe the thoughts in your head are your hell.

Maybe you have never lived until you have done something
for someone who could never repay you.

Maybe if you don't hear it with your own ears or see it
with your own eyes, you shouldn't repeat it.

Maybe you can heal your mind and body
with positive affirmations.

Maybe attracting your highest good in life is all that you need.

Maybe you're not listening to the messages from above.

Maybe you can let go of all the baggage of your past
that you have been lugging around for years.

Maybe your baggage keeps you from your true self.

Maybe we are all on a spiritual journey and don't know it.

Maybe you will never step forward and will stay
stuck where you are.

Maybe you should honor the place in you in
which the entire universe dwells.

Maybe you are in that place of you and
I am in that place of me and we are one.

Maybe my reality is my reality as long as it doesn't hurt anyone.

Maybe holding onto resentment is letting someone
live in my head rent free.

Maybe crying over the same thing over and over again
isn't the solution.

Maybe if you're doing the same thing over and over expecting
something to change, you need to change.

Maybe I am who I am and your approval isn't needed.

Maybe I am enough.

Maybe we can share without shame and that's what connects us.

Maybe learning to live life in the solution -
not the problem - is the answer.

Maybe time heals.

Maybe it's all about letting go and letting God!

Let Go, Let God

This was probably the hardest lesson that I had to learn. When people would tell me to let go, let God. It would stir an emotion inside of me. I would think to myself, *"how dare they say that to me, this is my child, I'm his Mother, I have every right to think and act the way I chose to when it concerns the wellbeing of my child"*.

I came to realize that our children are gifts from God; a Mother is a vehicle in which they come to us. In time, I came to realize that they weren't telling me not to love or care for my child, they were telling me that I was powerless over his disease and that I needed to surrender my control and will and that I should emotionally put my son in God's hands.

The day that I decided to let go, let God, was through meditation. The vision of my son lying in a casket came to me, I leaned into the casket and picked him up, I hugged him, God's hands reached out and I gently laid my son in the hands of God. As tears were running down my face a feeling came over me that my son would be ok.

Let go and let God may feel like you're letting go of the person that you love when in fact you're letting go of the disease who is in control of your loved one. Letting go is when you understand that you cannot control the outcome of their disease and that my friend is called acceptance.

"Listen, Lord Listen, Lord, a mother's praying low and quiet: listen, please. Listen what her tears are saying, see her heart upon its knees; lift the load from her bowed shoulders till she sees and understands, You, Who holds the world together, hold her problems in your hands." author unknown

<u>LETTING GO TAKES LOVE</u>

To let go does not mean to stop caring,
it means I can't do it for someone else.

To let go is not to cut myself off,
it's the realization I can't control another.

To let go is not to enable,
but allow learning from natural consequences.

To let go is to admit powerlessness, which means
the outcome is not in my hands.

To let go is not to try to change or blame another,
it's to make the most of myself.

To let go is not to care for,
but to care about.

To let go is not to fix,
but to be supportive.

To let go is not to judge,
but to allow another to be a human being.

To let go is not to be in the middle arranging all the outcomes,
but to allow others to affect their destinies.

To let go is not to be protective,
it's to permit another to face reality.

To let go is not to deny,
but to accept.

To let go is not to nag, scold or argue,
but instead to search out my own shortcomings and correct them.

To let go is not to adjust everything to my desires,
but to take each day as it comes and cherish myself in it.

To let go is not to criticize or regulate anybody,
but to try to become what I dream I can be.

To let go is not to regret the past,
but to grow and live for the future.

To let go is to fear less and love more.

And

To let go and to let God, is to find peace!

Author Unknown

Chapter 6

Healing Means Revealing!

Healing means "to restore to health or restore to spiritual wholeness" (*free dictionary.com*). Recovering from drug addiction or alcoholism is a healing process that not only heals a person's mind and body but typically brings them to a spiritual awakening. As loved ones we too need to go through our own healing process. If we don't get emotionally healthy and change our thought process and behavior then our loved one who is in recovery is at risk of being around us, as we may become toxic to them. Every time my son came home from a drug re-habilitation center, I would be on him, *"did you look for a job today, did you go to a meeting today, what did you do all day and who were you with?"* None of this was my business; I should have let him do his recovery his way and worked on mine because I became one of his triggers.

There is a twelve step process that was adapted by the Big Book that is a set of principles for recovery from addictive, compulsive, or other behavioral problems. One of the steps I feel that can help all of us heal is Step # 4. We made a searching and fearless moral inventory of ourselves. Observe our behavior, our thought process, and our part in the story.

I attend a weekly meeting called All Addictions Big Book Step Study (*I was addicted to saving my son from drugs*), although I don't have the allergy, I have experienced the steps as they are laid out in the big book with my step study sponsor and my higher power. Believe me when I tell you, it's a painful yet freeing process that I think everyone in society should do whether you have the allergy (*disease*) or not.

Throughout this process I have learned that I was often blaming others for things that happened in my life and my son's. I learned that while I was pointing my finger at everyone else's behavior that I wasn't paying attention to the three fingers that were folded back pointing at me. I too, have a part in the situation and that's why taking a moral inventory is simply looking at how we re-act or play into a situation, while we blame someone else for the end result. The only thing that we can get away with in life is the truth, as the saying goes "the truth will set you free".

"Healing means revealing that which is already enacted, what you set your heart upon must come about. If you seek validation of your wounds, you shall surely find that; yet if you seek, instead, confirmation of your inner strength and power, that you shall find as well." Doreen Virtue

My Healing Process

Over the ten years of dealing with my sons drug addiction, I read many books, one of the first books that I found was "**Ask and It is Given**" by Ester and Jerry Hicks. In the book, I came across an Emotional Scale. This was huge for my healing. The emotional scale numbers feelings from number one to twenty-two. I was shocked when I realized that I was at the bottom of the scale. I was number 22, living with fear, grief, depression and powerlessness.

For the first time in years my feelings were right smack in front of my face. I was devastated, *"how the hell did I allow myself to get this point?"* when I logically took a look at this, I realized that I had felt numb for years, not realizing my emotions.

56

I typed the emotional scale onto an 8 ½ x 11 piece of paper, framed it and put it on my desk so that I could monitor my feelings daily.

I would work on moving my emotions up the scale by concentrating on a feeling that was higher than the number that I was currently at. For example: I was #22, depressed (*sleeping my life away, in the fetal position*), I would concentrate on #17 -anger. By allowing myself to feel how angry I was, I was slowly moving up the scale. The key to this is to identifying and feel the emotion and release it.

Every day, I would review my emotional scale to identify where I was at in that particular moment. Eventually I was able to get myself to the top of the scale. I work hard at keeping myself between #1-Joy to #7-Contentment. I'm not perfect so there are days that I can slide right back down to emotions that I don't particularly care to feel.

I can honestly tell you that as tough as this work is, joy and contentment feel much better than living in fear and depression.

EMOTIONAL SCALE

1. Joy, knowledge, empowerment, freedom, love, appreciation
2. Passion
3. Enthusiasm, eagerness, happiness
4. Positive, expectation/belief
5. Optimism
6. Hopefulness
7. Contentment
8. Boredom
9. Pessimism
10. Frustration, irritation, impatience
11. Overwhelmed
12. Disappointment
13. Doubt
14. Worry
15. Blame
16. Discouragement
17. Anger
18. Revenge
19. Hatred
20. Jealousy
21. Insecurity, guilt, unworthiness
22. Fear, grief, depression, powerlessness

From the book "Ask and it is Given" by Ester and Jerry Hicks

I was intrigued by the book "**Angels 101**" by Doreen Virtue. I've always felt a connection to angels and this book introduces you to working and healing with them. I also bought Doreen's Arch Angel Oracle Cards and Messages from Angel cards so that I could do readings for myself.

Funny how things play out sometimes (*of course that's if you believe*). One day, I decided that I would do a reading for my son because he had been looking for a job, at least that's what he was leading me to believe. I shuffled the cards and the first three cards that fell out of the deck, I used for his reading.

I can't remember what all of the cards were but I do remember one that kept calling my attention. It was the Divine Order card, Archangel Raguel: "Everything is how it needs to be right now, look past the illusion, and see underlying order." I left the cards out to show him later in the day when he returned home.

On that particular day, I noticed that a billfold where I kept cash and would hide was missing. I thought to myself that maybe I moved it to a different location. I searched everywhere and when my family returned home that evening, I asked each of them if they had seen my billfold. They all said "no". The next morning, I began pulling draws and closets apart wondering what the heck I did my billfold. Here is where it gets a little weird.

As I'm anxiously searching throughout my house, the doorbell rang, I went downstairs to the front door, no one was there, I noticed the Angel card reading that I had left out and forgot to mention to my oldest son.

I reviewed the reading and that one card kept jumping out at me *"look past the illusion and see underlying order"*. I went back upstairs and resumed my search. This scenario happened three more times. I decided to take my search into my son's bedroom. Sitting on his bed was my little Maltese dog; she looked at me and then would look down at the corner of his bed. The doorbell rang again, and yet again, no one was there. Back up to my son's room and my dog would look at me, then look down at the corner of his bed. Finally, it dawned on me to lift the corner of his mattress, and guess what I found? Yes, my billfold with no money in it.

Call me crazy, but I believe that the Angels were working with me that day to lead me to the truth. You see, no one could ever have convinced me that my son would steal from me.

When I confronted my son, the tears flowed and he told me that he just borrowed the money and was going to replace the money the next day and put my billfold back where he found it, Funny how things play out.

Over the years I learned to meditate. I learned that when I pray to my higher power, I am asking for assistance and when I meditate I will often receive the answer that I have been looking for.

A friend recommended that I have a Reiki session, at the time; I had no knowledge of what Reiki was or how it was practiced. I did and loved it because for the first time in years, I had a little bounce back in my step, my heart didn't feel so heavy, and I was actually laughing and smiling. I loved it so much that I found a woman to mentor me and in March of 2006 I became a Shamballa Reiki Master.

Reiki is a limited connection to a small part of the total energy spectrum available for all enlightenment. Shamballa Reiki is a combination of two methods of healing that when used together, can be called upon to access universal energies. The idea of Shamballa is based on older Eastern practices.

Shamballa means spiritual warrior. In the practice of Shamballa, one goes through several levels of training. In each level, we learn new concepts about things such as basic goodness and learning to live your life with love and goodness. Part of the concept of Shamballa method is to be able to look inwards for the answers. Those who have achieved those answers can then take Shamballa precepts to help enlighten all of society. To be enlightened in this sense means to have an unlimited amount of compassion for those around you. The basic concept of universal goodness is practiced through meditation.

Chakras are balanced during the treatment. Chakra's are seven points of energy running along the spine. The Chakras can become blocked, making us feel out of sync, sick or out of balance. To me it's when I'm having a day that I just don't feel like myself and I'm not sick.

The seven Chakras are:

7th Chakra – purple in color and known as the Crown Chakra:

The 7th Chakra Is located at the top of our head. It is where we can connect directly to the God of our understanding, aligning to our higher self. The 7th Chakra is for spiritual wisdom.

6th Chakra- indigo in color and referred to as the third eye:

The 6th Chakra is located at the forehead. It is the Chakra for vision, knowledge and wisdom.

5th Chakra – blue in color:

The 5th Chakra is located in the throat; it gives us the ability to speak our truth. It is for clear communication.

4th Chakra – Green in color and is known as the Heart Chakra:

The 4th Chakra is located between the breasts and it is where we give and receive love.

3rd Chakra – Yellow in color:

The 3rd Chakra is located in the solar plexus. This Chakra gives us good judgment, a sense of who we are and it is also where we store our emotions.

2nd Chakra – Orange in color:

The 2nd Chakra is located below the navel. It's our sexuality and sensuousness. It is gives us the ability to connect to others.

1st Chakra – Red in color and is known as the Root Chakra:

The 1st Chakra is located in our private area and connects us to Mother Earth.

During the time I was training to become a Reiki Master, I finally found the courage to go to Al-Anon but looking back I wasn't ready to receive or understand the process because I went to the meetings with the intent to get the answer of how I could save my son from his addiction. I wanted answers damn it, and in my still sick mind; I didn't have time to *"keep coming back"*.

After Al-Anon, I started to go to AA meetings, I felt comfortable there because I didn't have to speak and I could listen to their stories. Attending these meetings gave me a better understanding of the disease and what they have endured. I remember one man in recovery talking and he said *"we alcoholics don't think like normal people, our brains are wired differently"*, I wanted to run up and thank him because I did not know that about the disease. From that night on, I would go to AA meetings and if I listened I would often receive a gift of understanding and I eventually started to hear the answer to my question of how I could save my son from this disease. I learned that only my son could save himself and only he could get to the root of his disease by peeling away the layers of his pain.

I finally realized that I needed to do some of the same work that I expected my son to do in his recovery. I needed to do my own recovery, therefore, I needed to begin healing my broken heart, get out of my depression, stop living in fear, and start to recover from the financial burden that I allowed his addiction to cause. I needed to take back my power so that I could become emotionally healthy again and learn to live in the solution, not in the problem.

I began to read books that were about healing, I read:

- **Awakening to Your Life's Purpose** by Echart Toole
  I learned about the pain body and the ego. Learning to let go of my ego is something that I work on all the time. Listening to my ego is as simple as insisting my husband take a right because I think we'll get to our destination quicker, when he wants to take a left.

- **The Power of Now** by Echart Toole
  I learned that I should live in the moment, appreciate it and feel it. Not to worry about yesterday or tomorrow because it is out of my control. *"Worry pretends to be necessary but serves no useful purpose."* Echart Toole

- **Voice of Knowledge** by Don Miguel Ruiz
  In this book, I realized that I wasn't a victim in my son's disease, although I played the role quite well. We can all create our own stories about whatever we chose but I have a choice if I fall victim to the situation or not.

- **The Instruction/Living the Life Your Soul Intended**
  by Ainslie McLeod
  I learned that I am an old soul.

- **Unfinished Business** by James Van Praagh
  I loved this book because it taught me that if I listen, I can connect to my spirits.

- **Too Busy Not to Pray** by Bill Hybels
  I went back to church for a while to help me through some of my spiritual healing.

- **The Gift of Change** by Marianne Williamson
  This taught me spiritual guidance for living my best life.

- **Beautiful Boy** by David Sheff
  This book gave me the insight that I wasn't alone.

- **You Can Heal Your Life** by Louise L.Hay
  I learned that my perception of myself isn't how people perceive me. I learned to do positive affirmations to stay in a positive state of mind.

- **The Seven Spiritual Laws of Success** by Deepak Chopra
  This book is a practical guide to the fulfillment of your dreams.

- **Things Are Going Great In My Absence** by Lola Jones
  How to let go and let the Divine do the heavy lifting. I love, love, love this book! I learned to take the story out and feel my emotions; I also learned to let things happen as they are meant to be.

Chapter 7

I recommend That You Learn To:

- **Listen instead of talk.**
  When I learned to be quiet, he gave me information about his usage when he would have a sober honest moment.
- **Breathe!**
  It's amazing how inhaling and exhaling can be calming and relaxing.
- **Listen to your gut, not your heart.**
  Our heart sometimes lies to us, because it's what we want to believe. My gut tells me the truth.

- **Let Go and Let God.**
  Hand your loved one over to the hands of the God of your understanding.
- **Live in the solution, not the problem.**
  Concentrating on the problem only manifests more negative energy.
- **Understand the difference between being supportive versus enabling.**
  It's a fine line.
- **Take back your power.**
  If you allow yourself to get caught up in your loved ones drama, you give away a bit of yourself.
- **Do not be your loved ones judge and jury.**
  It is not your right, period! If you have nothing positive to say then don't say anything at all. Instead, say the serenity prayer.
- **Connect with your higher power.**
  Having a spiritual awakening brings us to a much better place in life.
- **Do not engage in your loved ones drama.**
  It only creates more drama.

- **Learn the signs of substance abuse.**
  Write in a journal and over time, you'll learn his or her patterns.
- **Journaling.**
  Years ago I started writing a gratitude journal, I wouldn't allow myself to start my day until I wrote at least one thing that I was grateful for.
- **Learn that their recovery is their recovery and your recovery is your recovery.**
  Your loved one's recovery is their business, do them a favor and don't try to control it. Give yourself permission to get into your own recovery and heal.
- **Learn about the disease.**
  It will help you to understand your loved one's behavior.
- **Learn that you are as sick as your secret.**
  Find support from positive influences.
- **Learn that we all need each other.**
  Sharing without shame connects us.
- **Learn that you are dealing with the disease.**
  It may look like your loved one but the disease is controlling their mind and body.
- **Learn that when they tell you how or what they are using or drinking, it's typically double or triple the amount or stronger.**
  My son led me to believe that he was taking Oxycontins when in fact he was shooting Heroin into his veins.
- **Learn to let go of your fear.**
  Fear is a story that you can create in your head, control your thoughts and feelings by meditating, praying or sing a song.
- **Learn that drug addicts and alcoholics are selfish and can be the most convincing liars, manipulators and thieves.**
  It's all about them and they'll take whatever they want if you don't secure your valuables.

- **Learn that they will find or pay for clean urine to pass a drug test.**
  I had heard about a Mother who would give her child her urine so her child could pass her drug test and wouldn't break probation, talk about enabling. They can also buy clean urine on-line or take a pill to clean their urine before being drug tested. If they resist taking a urine test, more than likely they know that they won't pass it.
- **Learn the Serenity Prayer.**
  God grant me the serenity to accept that things that I cannot change; the courage to change the things that I can; and the wisdom to know the difference.
- **Learn that time heals, love heals and your Higher Power heals.**
- **Learn to live one day at a time.**
- **Learn to live in the solution, not the problem.**
- **Learn to live!**

<u>Closing</u>

My journey to find the answers to save my son was challenging to say the least. Looking back, it was because I didn't want to listen or hear what other people who had walked my walked had to say. I made that choice and it was a long hard lonely journey.

Reach out to people who have been in your shoes and listen to what they have to say, it may alleviate a lot of heartache for you. Go to meetings if you are willing to be open to the process to learn about co-dependency and enabling. In the big scheme of things, your story doesn't matter, but your well- being matters and your emotional health matters and you matter!

When I started to get emotionally healthy, twice a day, I would write in my journals. When I got up in the morning I wrote in my gratitude journal. I would write things such as: I am grateful for my health, I am grateful that I have a roof over my head. When I went to bed at night I wrote in my life experience journal, I would write about my day and document my son's behavior and mine.

Today I am grateful for the journey that I have experienced. A blessing can be a curse and a curse can be a blessing, the curse of addiction almost destroyed my family but in the end the curse became a blessing because my son, my family and I would not be who we are today, therefore, I have no regrets and I am grateful. Letting go of my secret gave me a voice and a passion to speak publicly and freely without shame about my son's addiction, his recovery and my journey of healing and learning. I choose to believe that nothing is a coincidence and that my son and I went through those horrible years so that we could help others. My son has been clean and sober since Mother's Day 2008, he is very involved in a 12 step program; he goes on commitments and sponsors other men in their recovery. I speak at various venues and write a weekly column six months of the year on co-dependency and enabling. I have Mom's in particular reach out to me constantly looking for the answer.

I believe in paying it forward, therefore, if you need someone to talk to, feel free to contact me at peelingtheonion@comcast.net.

"Gratitude unlocks the fullness of life.
It turns what we have into enough and more.
It turns denial into acceptance, chaos to order,
confusion to clarity.
It can turn a meal into a feast, a stranger into a friend.
Gratitude makes sense of our past,
brings peace for today
and creates a vision for tomorrow."
Melody Beattie quotes

May Your Faith and Strength Heal Your Heart!